Eagles

NorthWord Press
Chanhassen, Minnesota

DEDICATION
For Ray and Mary—Fellow eagle watchers and parents-in-law extraordinaire

Photography © 2001: W. Perry Conway: front cover; Robin Brandt: back cover, pp. 14-15; Henry H. Holdsworth/Wild by Nature: pp. 4, 11, 41; Jeff Foott: pp. 5, 43; Michael Quinton/Minden Pictures: p. 6; Lee Kline: pp. 8-9, 37; Michael H. Francis: pp. 12, 16, 32, 34, 42; Tom & Pat Leeson: pp. 18, 23, 28, 29, 44; Greg Baer: pp. 20-21; Dominique Braud/Dembinsky Photo Assoc.: pp. 24-25, 33; Anthony Mercieca/Dembinsky Photo Assoc.: p. 30; Alan G. Nelson/Dembinsky Photo Assoc.: pp. 38-39.

Illustrations by John F. McGee
Designed by Russell S. Kuepper
Edited by Barbara K. Harold

NorthWord Press
18705 Lake Drive East
Chanhassen, MN 55317
1-800-328-3895
www.northwordpress.com

Library of Congress Cataloging-in-Publication Data

Evert, Laura
    Eagles / Laura Evert ; illustrations by John F. McGee.
      p. cm. -- (Our wild world series)
    ISBN 1-55971-777-7 (soft cover)
    1. Eagles--Juvenile literature. [1. Eagles.] I. McGee, John F. ill. II. Title. III. Series.

  QL696.F32 E934 2001
  598.9'42--dc21

                                                    00-045571

Printed in Malaysia

10 9 8 7 6 5

Eagles

Laura Evert
Illustrations by John F. McGee

NorthWord Press
Chanhassen, Minnesota

HAVE YOU EVER wondered how the bald eagle got its name? The answer may not be what you think. The name actually comes from the Old English word "balde," which means "white." And when you look at the white-feathered head of a bald eagle, that certainly makes sense!

Eagles belong to the same family of birds that includes hawks and buzzards. Around the world there are about sixty different species (SPEE-sees), or kinds, of eagles that are divided into four groups. Sea eagles live near water and feed mostly on fish. Snake eagles live near marshes and, as you can guess, eat snakes and other reptiles. Crested eagles have pointed feathers that stand up on top of their head. Booted eagles (also called true eagles) have feathers on their legs that go all the way down to their feet.

Seeing a bald eagle is often a dream come true for many bird watchers.

Bald eagles are good parents that build sturdy nests for their young.

Eagles build their nest up high so they have a clear view
of their territory and hunting area.

Every continent except Antarctica is home to at least one species of eagle. Bald eagles belong to the group of sea eagles. They can be found almost everywhere in North America—from Alaska and Canada to northern Mexico, and in every other U.S. state except Hawaii. The only other eagle that can be found on this continent is the golden eagle, which is a booted eagle.

There are probably more golden eagles than any other kind of eagle in the world today. They can be found as far north as Alaska and Newfoundland, and south along the Rocky Mountains and Pacific Coast to central Mexico. A few golden eagles can be found in the Appalachian Mountains, south to North Carolina. They also live across most of Europe and Asia, south to northern Africa.

A habitat is a specific place in the environment where animals (or people) can live. Golden eagles prefer to live in remote, rugged areas such as mountains, ravines, deserts, and prairies. They make their nests on rocky ledges, in caves found on cliffs, or sometimes in tall trees that stand alone. A bald eagle's habitat is usually a wooded area along a river, stream, or lake shoreline.

Good habitat for bald eagles must include two things: tall trees in which they can build their nests, and fresh water where they can find plenty of fish for food. Although fish is the bald eagle's favorite meal, it also eats rabbits, squirrels, muskrats, birds, small rodents such as mice, and sometimes ducks and other waterfowl. Bald eagles also eat carrion (KARE-ee-un), or dead animals, that they find on the ground or along roadsides.

Pages 8-9: Golden eagles are always on the lookout for food. Their concentration is keen.

Golden eagles are excellent hunters, and do not eat as much carrion as do bald eagles. And although golden eagles do not eat fish, they eat many of the same animals that bald eagles eat, as well as foxes, crows, tortoises, and some snakes. They may even catch and eat skunks and wild goats!

The feathers on any bird are called its plumage (PLOO-mij). An adult bald eagle is easy to recognize with its white head and tail feathers. The rest of its plumage is dark brown. Golden eagles have goldish feathers on the back of their head and neck. The plumage on their body is rich brown.

An eagle has over 7,000 feathers on its head and body. Yet all those feathers combined weigh only about 1 pound (454 grams)!

Eagles
FUNFACT:

The bald eagle's scientific name is *Haliaeetus leucocephalus*. The golden eagle's scientific name is *Aquila chrysaetos*.

All birds clean their feathers often. It is called preening
and is a very important part of eagle life.

The eagle's body is designed perfectly for a bird that spends much of its time soaring above the trees or just over a lake's surface, looking for its next meal. Many of the bones in the wings and body of an eagle are completely hollow and filled with air. The entire skeleton of an eagle only weighs half as much as its feathers, about 8 ounces (227 grams).

The strong, heavy muscles that power the wings make up almost half of the bird's total weight. Female eagles are larger than male eagles. Adult female eagles weigh up to 14 pounds (6.3 kilograms). Males weigh about 7 to 10 pounds (3.2 to 4.5 kilograms). Eagles that live in northern regions are usually larger than those that live farther south.

The eagle's strong wings make it easy to navigate in the air. A bird may sometimes need to change direction very quickly.

An eagle's long, broad wings have wingtip feathers that can be moved individually, making the eagle extremely agile (AJ-il), or quick and light. These feathers are called primaries. When eagles fly, the primary feathers spread apart and bend up at the tips. By moving the primaries the eagle can easily control its flight direction. The top of the wing is made up of feathers called secondaries.

The eagle's rounded tail is made up of twelve feathers, each of which is 10 to 16 inches (25 to 40 centimeters) long.

Eagles molt, or lose and replace most of their feathers, once every year. All of the feathers are not lost at the same time—it happens gradually. It can sometimes take many months for the shed feathers to be replaced. The feathers on the eagle's head are replaced first.

Eagles can glide over long distances without ever flapping their wings. They use warm currents of air, called updrafts or thermals, to propel themselves upward. Then they either float downward at a long, gentle slope or spiral down in great circles. When they want to soar higher they simply glide into an updraft that lifts them. The wingspan of a female eagle, from tip to tip, can be 8 feet (2.4 meters) long. A male's wingspan is about 6.5 feet (2 meters) long.

When flying through the air eagles can reach speeds of up to 40 miles per hour (64 kilometers per hour). But it is their diving speed that is most useful. Eagles sometimes hunt for prey (PRAY), or the animals on which they feed, while soaring high in the air or perched in a tall tree or on a cliff. When they see something that looks like food they swoop down at speeds of over 100 miles per hour (160 kilometers per hour) and grab the prey with their claws. Then they fly away, carrying their prey to a place where they can eat it.

When prey animals are not plentiful, bald eagles search for carrion.
This helps keep their environment free of some diseases.

An eagle's talons and beak are made of keratin, the same material that makes up human hair and fingernails.

Eagles need good eyesight to help them locate prey. Both the golden's dark eyes and the bald's yellow eyes are extra sharp. The vision of an eagle is believed to be 6 to 8 times better than that of a human. Scientists who study animals are called zoologists (zoe-OL-uh-jists). They believe that an eagle in flight can see a rabbit on the ground from up to 2 miles (3.2 kilometers) away! That's why we use the phrase "eagle-eyed" to describe someone who is good at noticing things that others may miss.

Eagles have binocular (by-NOK-yoo-ler) vision, which means that they can see with both of their eyes at the same time. They also have monocular (muh-NOK-yoo-ler) vision, which means they can also see out of one eye at a time. Having both kinds of vision gives eagles a wide field of view. However, they can only move their eyes a little within the eye sockets, so they must turn their whole head to fully see from side to side.

Eagles also have the ability to see colors better than other birds and animals can. But the trade-off for being able to see in color is that eagles do not see well at night, so they hunt mostly in daylight.

After skimming the surface of a pond and grabbing onto a fish, the eagle holds it tightly until it is ready to eat.

In addition to a regular eyelid, eagles also have a transparent membrane that crosses each eye sideways. As it moves across the eye, the membrane cleans and moistens the eye about once every 5 seconds. It also helps protect the eye from being accidentally pecked by hungry chicks at feeding time.

The eyes are not the only part of a bald eagle that is yellow. Both bald and golden eagles have feet that are covered with bright yellow, scaly skin.

Each foot has four strong toes. Three toes point forward and one points backward. Eagles can tightly curl their toes together and use them to grasp objects like we do with our hands.

Each toe has a black talon, or claw, that is 2 inches (5 centimeters) long. The talons can be used as weapons, but they are mostly used for catching prey. When the eagle swoops down to catch a meal, the razor-sharp talons dig into the prey and hold it securely during the flight back to the nest or other feeding place.

Eagles
FUNFACT:

Eagles are found on U.S. coins and paper money. They are also found on postage stamps from around the world, including the U.S. and Canada.

The bald eagle's hooked beak is also bright yellow. A golden eagle's beak is gray with a yellow cere (SEAR). The cere is a waxy knob at the base of the beak where the bird's nostrils are located. An eagle's beak is about 3 inches (7.6 centimeters) long and is sometimes used as a weapon. It is sharp and strong, and is used to tear apart prey before the eagle eats it. Eagles do not chew their food. Instead, they rip it into chunks and swallow the pieces whole.

Bald eagles prefer to eat fish, especially the kinds that feed near the surface of the water, because they are easier to catch. They do not plunge or dive into the water to catch fish as do some other birds. Instead, they skim across the surface of the water, and when they see a fish that looks easy to catch they swing their legs down into the water and grab the fish with their powerful talons.

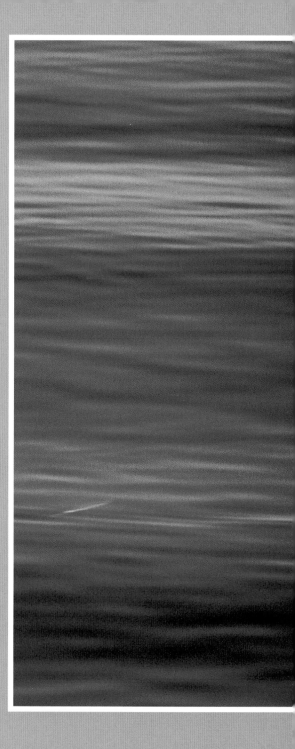

Eagles swing their feet forcefully down into the water so their talons can grab fish.

The bald eagle also has another way to get fish for dinner, but this method is more sly. When it sees another bird, such as an osprey (AH-spray), catch a fish, the eagle flies at the unsuspecting bird in a rush. The other bird, which is usually smaller and not as fierce, often drops the fish while trying to escape the eagle. The eagle then grabs the fish in midair and flies away to enjoy its stolen meal.

A high place such as a cliff ledge or a branch in a tree is the perfect place for an eagle to eat. High above the ground the eagle can keep a sharp lookout for predators (PRED-uh-tors), or enemies, while enjoying its meal. After the food is quickly torn into pieces and swallowed, it is stored in a pouch in the eagle's throat called the crop. The crop allows the bird to eat large amounts of food when there is plenty and store some for later, when hunting may be more difficult. The crop can hold as much as 1.5 pounds (680 grams) of meat.

When there are chicks to feed, the eagle still finds a perch where it can eat some of the food itself before giving the rest away to the hungry little mouths back at the nest.

A fresh salmon taken from the icy waters of a river makes a good meal for this eagle in winter.

Chicks must be fed several times a day,
which means many hunting trips for the parent.

Eagle nests are huge! Bald eagles usually select a tall, strong tree surrounded by some open space for a nest site. This makes it easier for the birds to come and go. Or the nest might be built in the crotch of a tree, usually just below the top. This gives the bird places to perch, and provides a good base on which to build the nest.

Many eagles build both a main nest and a second nest, often just a short distance away. Zoologists are not sure why they do this. It may be to confuse predators such as owls and raccoons that are a threat to the eggs and chicks. Or, the second nest may be built as a back-up to the main nest, in case the first nest is destroyed just before egg-laying. And if the adults are unable to produce eggs or chicks one year, they may try using the other nest the next year.

A bald eagle's nest is called an aerie (AIR-ee). The birds build and add to their nests by stacking sticks together. They carefully weave the sticks as though they were making a basket. The female does most of the work. A new nest that is 4 feet (1.2 meters) high and 5 feet (1.5 meters) across can be built in just a few days.

Eagles
FUNFACT:

The largest bald eagle nest on record measured almost 10 feet (3 meters) across and over 20 feet (6 meters) deep, and weighed over 4,000 pounds (1,800 kilograms).

The nest is usually lined with soft grasses and leaves to cushion the eggs. The nest's high edge prevents the chicks from tumbling out. More nesting material is added throughout the season to cover waste in the nest. Eagles are "messy" birds. They eat in the nest and do not throw out the left-overs!

Every year eagles repair damage to their nest and add more twigs and sticks. If a pair of eagles uses the same nest year after year, the nest may reach a height and weight so great that it topples the tree. An old nest that is reused many times may be over 8 feet (2.4 meters) across and weigh up to 2,000 pounds (907 kilograms)— about the same size as a small truck! Some eagle nests have lasted a hundred years.

After the adults make the nest improvements for the season, the female lays the eggs. Exactly when an eagle lays its eggs depends on where it lives. In southern regions like Florida, eagles may begin laying eggs as early as November, while eagles farther north do not usually lay eggs until April. Birds in the North wait until the frozen waterways begin to thaw because they must be able to find fish.

This pine makes a good tree for an eagle nest. It is tall and the limbs are strong.

Eagles sometimes build their nests on cliffs, like this one in Alaska.

Bald eagle eggs are incubated for about 35 days before the chicks are ready to hatch. Golden eagle eggs like these can take up to 45 days to hatch.

Bald eagles usually lay one or two eggs, occasionally even three eggs. Golden eagles lay up to four eggs, but two eggs is most common. A day or two passes between the laying of each egg. The eggs of the bald eagle are white. Golden eagle eggs are white too, but sometimes they have brown blotches on them.

After the eggs are laid, one adult sits on them almost all the time, especially during stormy or cold weather. The female spends the most time incubating the eggs, but the male takes a turn when she leaves the nest to hunt for food. Sometimes the male brings food to his mate while she sits on the eggs.

The eggs are gently turned every so often to provide even warmth. This prevents the embryo (EM-bree-oh), or developing chick, from sticking to the inside of the shell.

Before the chicks hatch, the adults can hear them calling out from inside their shell. Sometimes it takes a chick nearly a whole day to break out of its shell. It uses a little tooth on the end of the beak called an egg tooth, which soon falls off.

Since the eggs were laid at different times, they hatch a few days apart. The first hatchling out of its shell has the advantage and often wins the fight for food. Without enough to eat, the second chick sometimes does not survive. Stormy weather and disease are also dangers for chicks, and some years only 50 percent of all eagle chicks survive.

Eagle chicks are called eaglets. They have coats of soft, gray down. The eaglets are only about 4 inches (10 centimeters) long and may weigh just 2 ounces (60 grams).

Eagles
FUNFACT:

Eagles often nest within 100 miles (160 kilometers) of the place they were born. They usually mate for life, and can live to be over 30 years old.

Eaglets cry out for food almost as soon as they hatch.

For the first two weeks one adult is always at the nest to protect the chicks from harm and the cold. The male eagle usually brings them food. Sometimes the female does not allow him to eat at the nest with the rest of the family. The female gently places bits of food into the chick's mouth. As the eaglets grow, the parents provide protection and food— and shade on hot days.

By the end of four weeks the eaglets begin growing a darker down coat in place of the gray one. They are clumsy, but soon learn to stand. During this time both of the parents share hunting and feeding duties. Every three hours fresh food is brought to the nest to feed the ravenous, or very hungry, chicks.

This young, or immature, bald eagle stretches its wings to become stronger as it learns to fly from the nest.

This young bald eagle has found a good perch. It is learning to watch for prey on the ground below so it can hunt for itself.

Until now, the eaglets patiently waited while the adults tore up their food into small bits. After about eight weeks, the food is torn into larger pieces and the young eagles boldly snatch the food that is tossed in front of them.

At nine weeks old, the chicks are nearly full grown. They are active and noisy and constantly demand food. The eaglets also spend a lot of time jumping and flapping in the nest as they get ready to learn to fly. Finally, when they are ten to twelve weeks old they are ready to fledge, or leave the nest and fly for the first time. Their coats of down have been replaced by dark brown feathers.

Young golden eagles have a white tail with a dark brown band on the bottom edge and some white on their wings. Bald eagles do not have white feathers on their head or tail until they are about four or five years old. And that is when both kinds of eagles are ready to mate for the first time.

Eagles
FUNFACT:

Don't let the light weight of an eagle feather fool you. Pound for pound an eagle wing is as strong as the wing of an airplane!

Some eagles glide gracefully out of the nest on their first attempt to fly, but then struggle as they try to land on a perch. If an eaglet crashes to the ground during its early attempts at flight, the parents stay nearby. They call out to the young one, providing protection and encouragement until the excited young bird tries to fly again.

While learning to fly, young eagles still rely on their parents for food. Feeding may take place at a perch away from the nest. When they are twenty weeks old the young are nearly able to take care of themselves. In northern regions, it is almost time for migration out of the nesting territory to warmer areas. Some southern eagles move north to avoid the heat. Young eagles migrating for the first time usually have to travel farther to find a territory that is not already occupied by other eagles.

Young eagles stay with their parents even after they have grown to their full size. They separate when they migrate.

It is more common to see a golden eagle near the ground, because it hunts more land prey than the bald eagle.

Many golden eagles do not migrate at all if there is plenty of food in their territory. Adult bald eagles may only migrate as far as necessary to find an area with plenty of food. Golden eagles sometimes have a hunting territory of over 160 square miles (414 square kilometers). An adult bald eagle's territory is usually smaller than 10 square miles (26 square kilometers).

Most eagles, especially goldens, prefer to live away from other eagles, except for their mates. But in areas where there is plenty of food to go around it is not unusual to see many bald eagles living peacefully together. These eagles may even share food. In some parts of Alaska, up to 4,000 bald eagles may gather to feast on migrating salmon.

Eagles
FUNFACT:

The golden eagle is the national bird of Mexico. And even though Benjamin Franklin suggested the turkey, Congress made the bald eagle the national symbol of the United States in 1782.

When they must, eagles defend their territory in several ways. Sometimes they soar high in the air, circling their land for other birds to see. Other times they perch in the branches of the highest tree, keeping watch for intruders. When one eagle crosses into another's territory, the resident quickly charges and chases the intruder away. If a mated pair has claimed the territory, both the male and female defend it. It is common to see one eagle perched in a tree on one side of a lake and its mate perched in a tree on the opposite side.

As they watch for trespassers, the pair calls back and forth to each other. Bald eagles have a high-pitched, thin voice that seems weak for such a big bird. Their call sounds like a string of cackles, first going up and then down in pitch. Some people think it sounds like a giggle. Golden eagles are usually silent. When they do call, it sounds like a scream or high-pitched *"kee-kee-kee"* squeal.

Eagles
FUNFACT:

Sometimes the fish that an eagle grabs is so heavy that the eagle cannot immediately fly into the air. To build up speed before it takes off, the eagle can "row" across the water, using its wings as oars.

These parents are flying back to the nest with a freshly caught fish to feed the hungry eaglets.

Native Americans have great respect for both bald eagles and golden eagles. Some tribes considered the bald eagle to be equal to humans. Other tribes used eagle feathers in ceremonial costumes and celebrations, while still other tribes decorated only the bravest warriors with eagle feathers.

Eagles may live year-round in cold-weather climates as long as there is enough food.

At one time there were probably up to 500,000 bald eagles in North America. By 1963 there were less than 500 pairs of eagles in the lower U.S. Their survival was threatened in several ways, including hunting and loss of habitat. Big birds need big areas of land on which to find food and raise their young. As more and more people populated the continent, life became difficult for eagles. In 1967 the bald eagle was an endangered species.

The most severe threat to bald eagles was the use of a pesticide called DDT. People used it to kill mosquitoes and other insects. Since bald eagles mainly ate fish that ate the poisoned insects, the birds consumed large amounts of the poison. DDT would stay in the body of an eagle for many years. It caused the eggs to have thin, weak shells that would break as they were laid or when the female tried to incubate them. Because of this, very few new chicks were hatched for many years.

Eagles gather in the same area if prey is plentiful.

In the air or on the ground, the white head of an
adult bald eagle makes it easy to identify.

In 1972 people were no longer allowed to use DDT, and gradually eagles were able to recover. Finally, in 1995, the bald eagle population in all of the lower 48 states had increased enough for them to be listed as threatened instead of endangered. Fortunately, the golden eagle did not suffer as much DDT poisoning since its prey is mostly grass-eating animals.

Today there are about 5,800 pairs of bald eagles in the lower U.S. and over 100,000 bald eagles in Alaska and Canada. Environmental groups are working together to set aside protected land for bald and golden eagles to use as their territories. Zoologists are finding ways to improve the survival rate of eaglets. And people are constructing platforms on which eagles can build their nests and raise their young.

With so many people working hard for eagle survival, we can hope that future generations will always be able to watch eagles soar and glide across the open sky.

Eagles
FUNFACT:

If you want to see large numbers of bald eagles, a good place to go is near Haines, Alaska. Or you can attend a bald eagle festival in cities like Rock Island, Illinois; Dubuque, Iowa; or Emery, Texas.

Internet Sites

You can find out more interesting information about eagles and lots of other wildlife by visiting these web sites.

http://endangered.fws.gov/kids/index.html	U.S. Fish and Wildlife Service
www.animal.discovery.com	Discovery Channel Online
www.audubon.org	Audubon Society
www.eaglestock.com/kidspage.htm	Bald Eagle Kids Page
www.EnchantedLearning.com/subjects/birds	Disney Online
www.kidsgowild.com	Wildlife Conservation Society
www.kidsplanet.org	Defenders of Wildlife
www.nationalgeographic.com/kids	National Geographic Society
www.nwf.org/kids	National Wildlife Federation
www.state.ak.us/adfg/notebook/notehome.htm	Alaska Dept. of Fish and Game
www.tnc.org	The Nature Conservancy
www.worldwildlife.org	World Wildlife Fund

Index

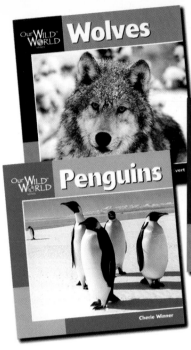

ALLIGATORS
AND CROCODILES
ISBN 1-55971-859-5

BISON
ISBN 1-55971-775-0

BLACK BEARS
ISBN 1-55971-742-4

CARIBOU
ISBN 1-55971-812-9

CHIMPANZEES
ISBN 1-55971-845-5

COUGARS
ISBN 1-55971-788-2

DOLPHINS
ISBN 1-55971-776-9

EAGLES
ISBN 1-55971-777-7

GORILLAS
ISBN 1-55971-843-9

HAWKS
ISBN 1-55971-886-2

LEOPARDS
ISBN 1-55971-796-3

LIONS
ISBN 1-55971-787-4

LIZARDS
ISBN 1-55971-857-9

MANATEES
ISBN 1-55971-778-5

MONKEYS
ISBN 1-55971-849-8

MOOSE
ISBN 1-55971-744-0

ORANGUTANS
ISBN 1-55971-847-1

PENGUINS
ISBN 1-55971-810-2

POLAR BEARS
ISBN 1-55971-828-5

PRAIRIE DOGS
ISBN 1-55971-884-6

SEA TURTLES
ISBN 1-55971-746-7

SEALS
ISBN 1-55971-826-9

SHARKS
ISBN 1-55971-779-3

SNAKES
ISBN 1-55971-855-2

TIGERS
ISBN 1-55971-797-1

TURTLES
ISBN 1-55971-861-7

WHALES
ISBN 1-55971-780-7

WHITETAIL DEER
ISBN 1-55971-743-2

WILD HORSES
ISBN 1-55971-882-X

WOLVES
ISBN 1-55971-748-3

See your nearest bookseller, or order by phone 1-800-328-3895

NORTHWORD PRESS
Chanhassen, Minnesota